EVERYONE LOVES
PARIS

BY LESLIE JONATH

INTRODUCTION

BY LESLIE JONATH

I lived in Paris as a child and have loved it ever since. There are as many reasons to love Paris as there are people who love it. A city of visual and sensual pleasures, Paris is a place of light, color, texture, and mood that has inspired art, artists, and art movements with all its grandeur. Even if you don't consider yourself an artist, Paris makes you appreciate the art of living.

In curating the illustrations for this book, I endeavored to include images of beloved landmarks, such as Notre Dame and the Sacré-Coeur Basilica (and so many Eiffel Towers!), but also portraits of the small details that make Paris so lovely: leafy trees in a small neighborhood park; laughter and music emanating from bistros; the soft glow of a bridge over the Seine at night; a woman walking through Place des Vosges; or a patisserie window filled with chocolate cakes. This book also features Parisians—from café-goers and lovers to bicyclists and dog walkers—and is punctuated with French words and expressions.

In all seasons and in all weather, Paris is as much an emotion or state of being as it is a geographical place. Because everyone loves Paris in their own special way, gathering these images was like peering into a collection of intimate moments—small love affairs with the City of Light.

As an art form, illustration poignantly expresses this love through the artist's hand. Here you will find tributes from artists around the world expressing a multitude of styles and perspectives. Flipping through the pages of this book is like a wandering through Paris's streets and geography—a meander where you might stumble on something wonderful and surprising. Maybe you'll recognize some of your own passions within these pages—like a tiny detail or idea that recalls your love for this magical city.

The writer Ernest Hemingway declared, "If you are lucky enough to have lived in Paris as a young man, then wherever you go for the rest of your life, it stays with you, for Paris is a movable feast." My hope is that *Everyone Loves Paris* will serve as your very own moveable feast.

EINLEITUNG

VON LESLIE JONATH

Ich habe als Kind in Paris gelebt, und seitdem liebe ich diese Stadt. Es gibt genauso viele Gründe, sie zu lieben wie Menschen, die dies tun. Die Stadt ist ein einziges visuelles und sinnliches Vergnügen, ein Ort des Lichts, der Farben und Stimmungen, der durch seine Großartigkeit sowohl Kunst, Künstler als auch Kunstbewegungen inspirierte. Selbst wenn man sich nicht als Künstler versteht, lernt man durch Paris, die Kunst des Lebens zu schätzen.

Ich war bei der Auswahl der Bilder für dieses Buch darum bemüht, neben den vielbewunderten Wahrzeichen der Stadt wie Notre Dame, Sacré-Cœur (und ganz vielen Eifeltürmen!) auch jene kleinen Details miteinzubeziehen, die Paris so liebenswert machen: grüne Bäume in einem kleinen Park; Bistros, aus denen Gelächter und Musik dringen; der sanfte Schein einer Brücke über der Seine bei Nacht; eine Frau beim Überqueren des Place des Vosges; oder die mit Schokoladenkuchen gefüllte Auslage einer Patisserie. Natürlich dürfen auch die Pariserinnen und Pariser nicht fehlen – von Cafébesuchern und Liebenden bis hin zu Fahrradfahrern und Hundebesitzern. Alles untermalt von französischen Worten und Ausdrücken.

Paris bietet bei jeder Jahreszeit und jedem Wetter intime Momente, da alle Menschen diese Stadt auf ihre eigene Art und Weise lieben. Sie ist gleichermaßen ein Gefühlzustand wie ein geografischer Ort. Diese Bilder zusammenzustellen, war, als blicke man in eine Sammlung kleiner Liebesgeschichten mit der Stadt des Lichts.

Die Illustration als Kunstform vermag durch die Hand eines Künstlers diese Liebe auf den Punkt zu bringen. Sie werden hier auf Bilder von Künstlern aus aller Welt stoßen, die mit unterschiedlichen Stilen und Perspektiven die Stadt würdigen. Wenn Sie durch die Seiten blättern, werden Sie sich fühlen, als würden Sie selbst durch die Straßen und über die Plätze von Paris streifen – ein Rundgang, bei dem Ihnen vielleicht etwas Wunderschönes und Überraschendes begegnet. Vielleicht werden Sie in diesem Buch einige Ihrer Leidenschaften wiedererkennen – ein kleines Detail zum Beispiel oder ein Gedanke, der Ihnen Ihre Liebe an diese magische Stadt wieder in Erinnerung ruft.

Der Schriftsteller Ernest Hemingway hat einmal gesagt: „Wenn man das Glück hat, als junger Mann in Paris gelebt zu haben, bleibt die Stadt für immer bei einem, egal wohin man auch geht, denn Paris ist ein Fest fürs Leben." Meine Hoffnung ist, dass *Everyone Loves Paris* zu Ihrem persönlichen Fest fürs Leben wird.

INTRODUCTION

PAR LESLIE JONATH

Enfant j'ai vécu à Paris et depuis lors je l'ai toujours aimé. Les raisons d'aimer Paris sont tout aussi nombreuses que les gens qui l'aiment. Paris ville des plaisirs visuels et sensuels, est un lieu de lumière, couleur, texture et ambiance dont la splendeur a inspiré l'art, les artistes et les courants artistiques. Même si vous ne vous percevez pas comme un artiste, Paris vous fait apprécier l'art de vivre.

En rassemblant les illustrations pour ce livre, je me suis attachée à inclure des images des monuments préférés comme Notre Dame et la basilique du Sacré-Cœur (et tellement de Tours Eiffel !), ainsi que des illustrations de petits détails qui font tout le charme de Paris : des feuillages dans un petit parc de quartier ; les rires et la musique émanant des bistros ; le doux reflet d'un pont sur la Seine le soir ; une femme qui travers la Place des Vosges ou la vitrine d'une pâtisserie remplie de gâteaux au chocolat. Ce livre qui montre aussi des Parisiens, dans des cafés, des amoureux, des cyclistes et des gens qui promènent leur chien, est ponctué de mots et d'expressions en français.

Au rythme des saisons et par tous les temps Paris offre des moments intimes parce que tout le monde aime Paris chacun à sa manière. Paris est tout autant une émotion ou un état d'esprit qu'un lieu géographique. Le fait de réunir ces images m'a donné l'impression de parcourir une collection de petites histoires d'amour avec la Ville Lumière.

En tant qu'expression artistique, l'illustration exprime de façon poignante cet amour à travers la main de l'artiste. Vous trouverez ici les hommages d'artistes du monde entier exprimant une multitude de styles et de points de vue. Parcourir les pages de ce livre c'est un peu comme flâner le long des rues et de la géographie de Paris, un méandre où vous pourriez tomber sur quelque chose de merveilleux et inédit. Vous reconnaîtrez peut-être certaines de vos passions au long de ces pages, par exemple un petit détail ou une idée qui vous rappellera votre amour pour cette ville magique.

L'écrivain Ernest Hemingway a dit un jour « si vous avez eu la chance d'avoir vécu à Paris pendant votre jeunesse, où que vous alliez par la suite, vous ne l'oublierez jamais car Paris est une fête ». Mon souhait c'est que *Everyone Loves Paris* (Tout le monde aime Paris) sera pour vous aussi une fête visuelle.

la Petite Patisserie

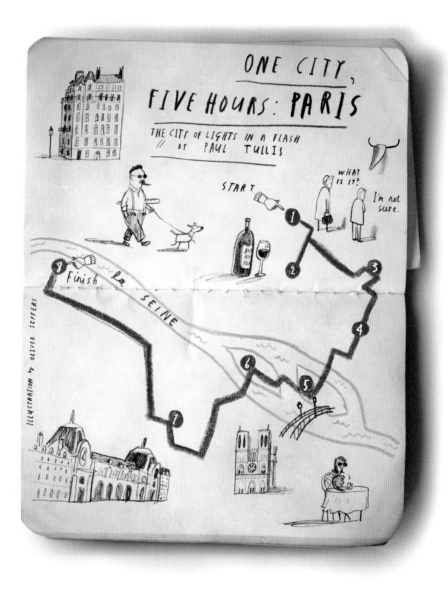

ONE CITY,
FIVE HOURS: PARIS

THE CITY OF LIGHTS IN A FLASH // BY PAUL TULLIS

START

WHAT IS IT?

I'm not sure.

Finish

La SEINE

ILLUSTRATION by OLIVER JEFFERS

I did try to study french.

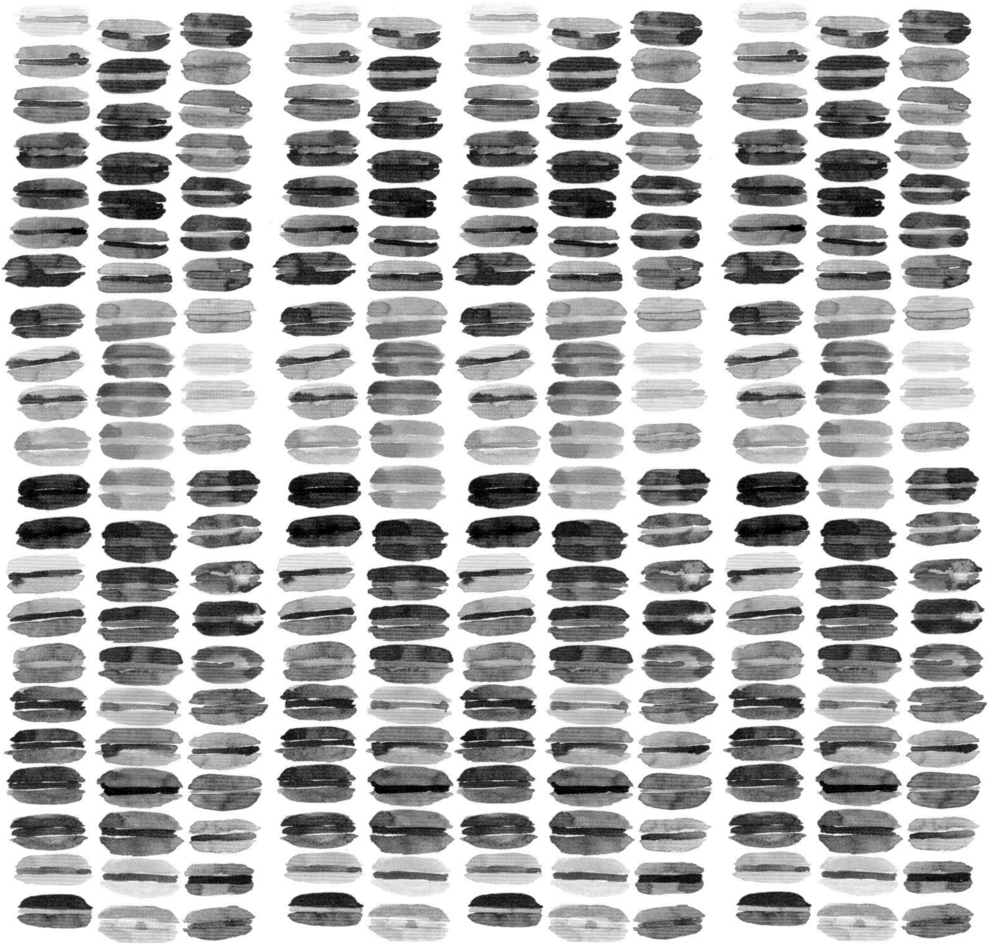

PARIS

HMM, WHAT SHALL I WEAR TODAY?

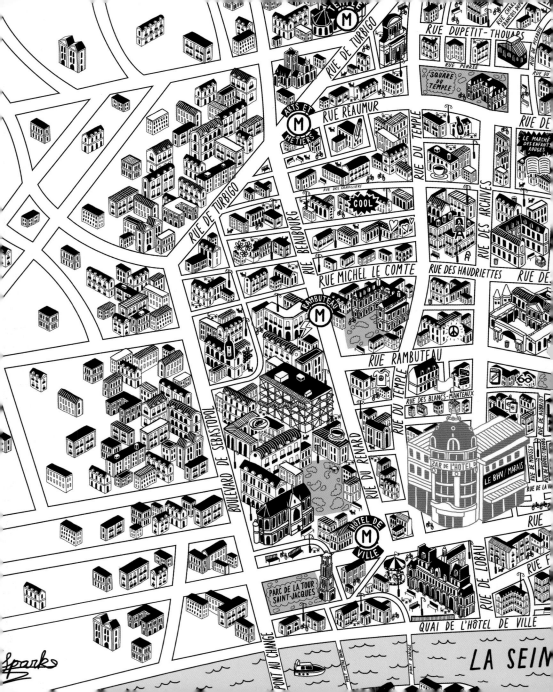

d'aujourd'hui ne se
payent qu'en
janvier.

MADE IN FRANCE

LE CONSULAT

Ma son Catherine
à la Mère Catherine

Boula

montmatre
paris

Café rouge

Métro

Metropolitain

Paris

99

NOTRE-DAME Cathedral

GARGOYLES

South ROSE window
window

Flying
Buttresses

Pont Neuf + the Seine
Pont Neuf (New Bridge) is the oldest bridge in PARIS
— completed in 1607

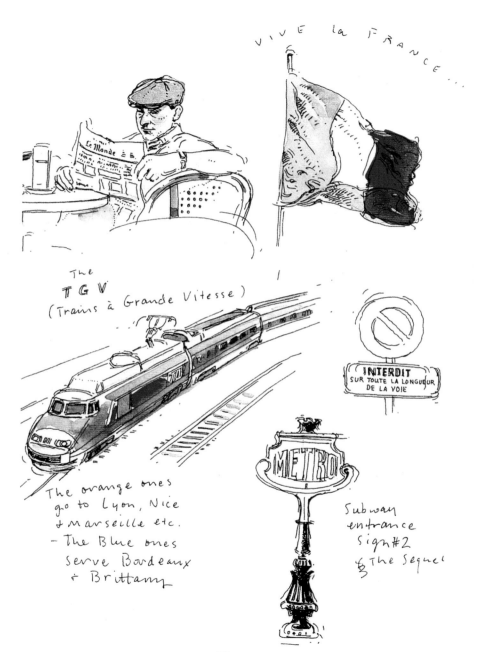

VIVE la FRANCE...

The
TGV
(Trains à Grande Vitesse)

INTERDIT
SUR TOUTE LA LONGUEUR
DE LA VOIE

The orange ones
go to Lyon, Nice
+ Marseille etc.
- The Blue ones
serve Bordeaux
+ Brittany

METRO

Subway
entrance
sign #2
& The Sequel

Paris, Je T'aime

ARTIST CREDITS

2
Clare Caulfield
© Clare Caulfield.

4
Bonnie Dain
© Bonnie Dain / Lilla Rogers Studio.
www.lillarogers.com.

8–9
Amy Borrell
© Amy Borrell.

10
Kevin Lucius
© Kevin Lucius.

11
Emma Block
© Emma Block.

12
Laura Amiss
© Laura Amiss.
Originally for Papyrus.

13
Laura Amiss
© Laura Amiss.
Originally for Papyrus

14–15
Matte Stephens
© Matte Stephens.

16
Matte Stephens
© Matte Stephens.

17
Matte Stephens
© Matte Stephens.

18
Gattobravo
© Gattobravo.

19
Gattobravo
© Gattobravo.

20
Emma Block
© Emma Block.

21
Emma Block
© Emma Block.

22–23
Dominique Corbasson
© Dominique Corbasson / cwc.i.com.

24
Oliver Jeffers
© Oliver Jeffers.
Originally for United Airlines.

25
André François
© 2014 Artists Rights Society (ARS),
New York / ADAGP, Paris.
Originally published in
The Magic Currant Bun.

26–27
Dominique Corbasson
© Dominique Corbasson / cwc.i.com.

28
Emma Block
© Emma Block.
Originally for Rosehip Cards.

29
Jayde Fish
© Jayde Fish.

30
Dominique Corbasson
© Dominique Corbasson / cwc.i.com.

32
Beth Adams
© Beth Adams.

LESLIE JONATH

Leslie Jonath lived in Paris as child and has been in love with the city ever since. She is the author of numerous books including *Postmark Paris*, *Bee & Me*, *At the Farmer's Market with Kids*, *The Dictionary of Extraordinary Ordinary Animals*, and *Give Yourself a Gold Star* as well as the blog *Feed Your People: Food to Gather Around*. In addition to writing books, she is also the founder of Connected Dots Media, a content packaging company that creates beautiful illustrated books and content on food, cooking, art and design, pop culture, and other odd and eclectic topics. She lives in San Francisco. www.connecteddotsmedia.com.

Leslie Jonath lebte als Kind in Paris und liebt seitdem die Stadt. Sie ist Autorin zahlreicher Bücher, unter anderem von *Postmark Paris*, *Bee & Me*, *At the Farmer's Market with Kids*, *The Dictionary of Extraordinary Ordinary Animals* und *Give Yourself a Gold Star* sowie des *Blogs Feed Your People: Food to Gather Around*. Neben ihrer Arbeit als Buchautorin ist sie Inhaberin des Redaktionsbüros Connected Dots Media, das wunderschöne Bildbände herstellt, die sich mit Essen, Kunst und Design, Popkultur sowie anderen ungewöhnlichen und bunten Themen befassen. Sie lebt in San Francisco. www.connecteddotsmedia.com.

Enfant, Leslie Jonath a vécu à Paris et depuis son amour pour la ville ne s'est jamais démenti. Elle est l'auteur de nombreux livres dont *Postmark Paris* (*Cachet de la poste à Paris*), *Bee & Me* (*Bee et moi*), *At the Farmer's Market with Kids* (*Au marché avec les enfants*), *The Dictionary of Extraordinary Ordinary Animals* (*Le dictionnaire des animaux ordinaires extraordinaires*) et *Give Yourself a Gold Star* (*Donnez-vous une étoile en or*) de même que le blog *Feed Your People: Food to Gather Around* (*Nourissez vos gens : aliments à rassembler*). Outre le fait d'écrire des livres, elle est aussi la fondatrice de Connected Dots Media, une société de conception packaging qui crée de beaux livres illustrés parlant de nourriture, cuisine, art et design, culture pop et autres sujets originaux et éclectiques. Elle habite à San Francisco. www. connecteddotsmedia.com.

ACKNOWLEDGMENTS

This project was a lovely collaboration and I am most grateful to the artists who graciously accepted the invitation to share their work. I am also thankful to the talented group at teNeues Publishing, including my wonderful editor Victorine Lamothe and extraordinary designer Allison Stern, as well as to Christina Burns and Audrey Barr for first acquiring the project. I would also like to extend a special thank-you to my team: curator Debra Lande for bringing her keen sensibility to the project; to researcher Rachel Piltch; editorial assistant Jessica Goss; and to Laurel Leigh for keeping everything on track always. *Merci a tous !*

DANKSAGUNG

Dieses Buch ist das Ergebnis einer wundervollen Zusammenarbeit mit den Künstlern, denen ich äußerst dankbar bin, dass sie der Einladung gefolgt sind, ihr Werk mit uns zu teilen. Mein Dank gilt gleichermaßen dem talentierten Team von teNeues, darunter Victorine Lamothe, meiner wunderbaren Lektorin, der außergewöhnlichen Grafikerin Allison Stern sowie Christina Burns und Audrey Barr, die dieses Buch in ihr Programm aufgenommen haben. Ein besonderer Dank geht auch an mein Team: an Debra Lande a, meine Kuratorin, für ihr Feingefühl bei diesem Buch; an Rachel Piltch, die für die Recherchearbeiten verantwortlich war, an Jessica Gross, Lektoratsassistentin, und an Laurel Leigh, die stets alles nachverfolgte und im Auge behielt. *Merci a tous !*

REMERCIEMENTS

Ce projet fut un bel exemple de collaboration et je suis particulièrement reconnaissante envers les artistes qui ont accepté aimablement notre invitation de partager leur travail. Je tiens également à remercier l'équipe talentueuse de teNeues Publishing, dont fait partie ma merveilleuse rédactrice Victorine Lamothe et une conceptrice extraordinaire, Allison Stern, de même que Christina Burns et Audrey Barr qui sont à l'origine de l'acquisition du projet. Je voudrais aussi dire un grand merci à mon équipe : ma conservatrice Debra Lande pour avoir apporté sa vive sensibilité à ce projet ; mon chercheur, Rachel Piltch ; mon assistante d'édition, Jessica Goss et Laurel Leigh pour toujours garder le cap. *Merci à tous !*